About Earth

Pauline Cartwright

Contents

Earth

Hi! I'm Zudu, your tour guide for Earth. We're about to enter Earth's **solar system**. Are you ready for a quick spin around Earth? Just don't let the humans see you!

I'm here to answer all your questions about Earth. Ask away!

Earth is the third planet from the Sun. Earth is the only planet that humans know about that has **liquid** water on it.

Earth's solar system includes the Sun and everything that travels around it.

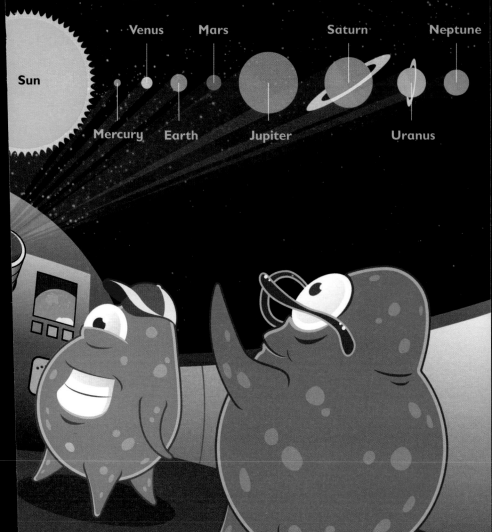

Sun

Venus   Mars   Saturn   Neptune

Mercury   Earth   Jupiter   Uranus

Earth's Gravity

What is gravity?

Gravity surrounds Earth. It is a strong **force** pulling all objects toward the middle of Earth. Without gravity, everything would float away from Earth!

ZUDU'S EARTH TOURS

Gravity keeps all people on Earth!

Earth's moon also has gravity, but its gravity is not as strong as Earth's gravity. That's why astronauts on the Moon moved with big, floaty steps!

Gravity is even linked to the movements of the sea, and that's where we are headed next!

Water on Earth

How much water is on Earth?

There is a *huge* amount of water on Earth. Water covers more than 70% of the Earth's surface.

The oceans make up most of Earth's water. Water is also found in rivers, lakes, and ice.

The longest river on Earth is the Nile, in Africa.

If all the ice in the world melted, the seas would rise by about 230 feet (70 meters). Many places on Earth would be flooded.

Let's take a closer look at the sea.

Why is the sea salty?

Much of the salt in the sea comes from rocks on the land. River water runs over rocks that **contain** salts, so the river water becomes slightly salty. The river then flows into the ocean. The ocean becomes more and more salty!

There is a salt lake on Earth called the Dead Sea. It is the saltiest body of water on Earth. This is because the rocks on the mountains around it are salty. The Dead Sea has so much salt in it that you can float without even trying!

Where do humans find water to drink?

Most of the water on Earth is salt water. But humans on Earth cannot drink this water. They need to drink water that is not salty. This water can be found in lakes, rivers, and streams. It can also be frozen or be found under the ground.

The fresh water found in lakes, streams, and rivers has a small amount of salt in it, but people can still drink it.

People make dams and lakes to catch rain water or river water.

Dry Places on Earth

Where is the driest place on Earth?

Put on your snow clothes because we are off to Antarctica. Almost all of Antarctica is covered with ice. But it is the driest place on Earth!

Antarctica

• South Pole

Antarctica's Dry Valleys have had no rainfall for more than two million years! It's very cold in the Dry Valleys. No living things can **survive** there.

Parts of the Dry Valleys have lakes under the snow and ice, but no rainfall.

Let's go somewhere warmer!

13

A warm desert with no rain

The Atacama Desert in South America is also very, very dry. This desert gets very little rain. Some parts of the Atacama Desert have had no rain for 400 years. Some parts in the desert have never had rain!

ZUOU'S EARTH TOURS

South America

Atacama Desert

Even though the Atacama Desert is very dry, some animals still live there. These include birds, lizards, and mice.

Sand

Where does sand come from?

Sand grains are very hard. This is because these sand grains were once rock. Rocks are broken up and turned into sand by the wind and water. This takes many, many, many millions of years to happen!

Water can slowly break down rock over time.

Low hills of sand are called dunes. Wind can move sand dunes.

The Sky

Why is the sky blue?

Light from the Sun is made up of all the colors of the rainbow. Most of the Sun's light passes straight through Earth's **atmosphere**, except for blue light. Blue light is scattered around the sky. So, when you look at the sky, you see all this blue light!

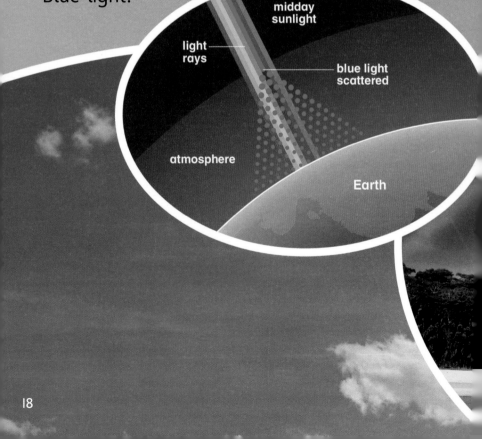

midday sunlight

light rays

blue light scattered

atmosphere

Earth

When can you see rainbows?

The colors of the rainbow are red, orange, yellow, green, blue, indigo, and violet. To remember their order, think of this name: ROY G. BIV. You can see rainbows when there are drops of water in the air and the Sun is low in the sky. A rainbow appears when the Sun's light shines through the raindrops.

Why are sunsets and sunrises red?

When the Sun rises and sets,
the sky is a red, orange, or pink color.

At sunset or sunrise, the Sun is lower in the sky, so its light must travel farther to get to Earth. Also, it must travel through more of Earth's atmosphere. This means more of the light is scattered, and the Sun looks less bright. This also means that most of the blue light is so scattered now, it doesn't even reach the Earth. So, you see the red and orange colors!

sunset

light rays

light scattered out

atmosphere

Earth

Any other questions about Earth? Even if they are tricky!

Thunder and Lightning

What causes thunder and lightning?

What's that? It's a thunderstorm. Can you hear the thunder and see the lightning?

Thunderstorms happen a lot in spring and summer.

Thunderstorms happen when there is a lot of warm air near the ground. As this air rises, it becomes cooler and turns into heavy, dark clouds, full of ice and raindrops. The rumbling sound of thunder is when the warm air meets the cooler air.

When there is thunder, there is lightning. Lightning is an electric, hot spark. Lightning happens when lots of small bits of ice in a storm cloud bump into each other. There is a lot of electricity in the storm clouds.

Lightning does not often hit the ground, but when it does, it can strike trees and buildings and cause fires.

The Wind

What makes the wind?

Wind is made because the Sun warms Earth's air. Warm air goes up. As warm air goes up, a rush of cold air moves in under it. This makes wind.

Sun

warm air rises

wind

land

cold air

water

Wind moves over land and sea. The wind that moves over the land is often warmer than the wind over the sea. This is why most of Earth's coldest winds come in from the sea!

Remember: warm air goes up! That's what makes hot air balloons move upward.

Earthquakes and Volcanoes

What makes an earthquake?

Earth is made up of rocks and liquid. The top part of Earth is made of huge plates of rock. Just under these plates is melting, **oozing** rock. The huge plates move slightly on top of the melting rocks.

The collapsed Cypress Freeway in Oakland, California, after the 1989 Loma Prieta earthquake.

When the edges of plates push past each other, they shake and rumble. This is an earthquake.

huge rock plate

huge rock plate

melted rock

What makes a volcano erupt?

We know about Earth's huge plates and melting rocks. But below them, there are rocks that have melted into very hot liquid. This liquid rock is called magma.

lava

volcano

magma

Sometimes, the magma bursts up through the earth, in between the huge plates. This is a volcano erupting!

Magma is the name of melted rock under the ground. Lava is the name for magma that is on top of the ground.

Phew, it's hot here!

Earth Quiz

Well, that's the end of our tour of Earth! We'll come back another time. There is still so much to learn!

Now, what did **you** learn about Earth? Try this quiz!

 Why can't you drink most of Earth's water?

 What is the force that stops you from floating off into space?

 What sound can be heard when warm air meets cool air?

 What is the name of liquid rock under the ground?

Glossary

atmosphere   the gases surrounding Earth

contain   to have as a part of something

force   a power, a strength

liquid   a kind of fluid, such as water

oozing   slowly moving, squeezing through

solar system   the Sun and everything in space that travels around it

survive   to remain alive